THE ENEMY OF EVERYTHING

THE ENEMY OF EVERYTHING

MICHAEL JONES

atmosphere press

TABLE OF CONTENTS

To Tracy, Madeline, Jake, Dylan & Luke -

You are the magic in my Reality

EPIGRAPH

War, famine, disease, genocide. death, in a million different forms, often painful and protracted for the poor individual wretches involved. What god would so arrange reality to predispose its creations to experience such suffering, or be the cause of it in others? What master of simulations or arbitrator of a game would set up the initial conditions to the same pitiless effect? God or programmer, the charge would be the same: that of near-infinitely sadistic cruelty; deliberate, premeditated barbarism on an unspeakably horrific scale.

-Ian M. Banks, *Matter*

Imagination is the only weapon in the war against reality.

-Lewis Carroll, *Alice in Wonderland*

3

REALITY RULES

Of all the people living now,
and all who've ever been,
Reality's rules and all its ways
links every human being as kin.
Since our first blink of imagination
we've sought the reasons we exist,
yet all the thinkers
and artists
and gurus of God,
have left us fumbling with a list:

Reality is a psychopath,
seeking ends without regard,
to the human carnage fostered
in its wake of blood and char.
Or Reality's just our dream,
or it's all someone else's dream,
but if so, then who is sleeping,
and will they wake from this dream scheme?
Or Reality is God,
projected from the supreme mind,
but why would God need human beings,
and if so, why purpose blind?
Or Reality is an illusion,
painted between the eyes and brain,
perception generating pictures,
imagined pleasure
made up pain.
Or Reality is a simulation,
used to distract or to control.
Then who are these architect masters?
Who made them
and what's their goal?
Or Reality's a prison sentence,

we're guilty of some unknown crime,
forced to live outside of infinity,
suffering the loss that comes with time.
Or Reality is a joke,
a cosmic jester's little game,
just a source of entertainment
with only funny as its aim.
Or Reality is Heaven,
we're in the end all
be all place.
Could be that all dimension's beings
strive to join this human race.
Or Reality is Hell,
we're born, we die,
repeat forever,
this place is filled with being's losers
with zero hope left whatsoever.
Or Reality is a gift,
one life's reward for doing well,
there's something special in this fate,
reserved for souls who all excel.
Or Reality is a test,
to see what direction we go next,
we're being judged for all we do,
wandering through our lives perplexed.
Or Reality is absurd,
and seeking why's a pointless act,
there is still some higher power,
but it's insane
and warped
and cracked.
Or Reality is an accident,
and there is nothing more to say,
it's some impossible natural phenomenon,
no why's at all
just numbered days.

So, there are these plus other paths,
and every one could be the truth,
we can ponder for millennia
without a single shred of proof.

Instead, it's time for revolution,
to radically rethink why we're here,
what kind of asylum are we running
living this long with why not clear?

Yes, an uprising's in order,
since all the wondering has failed,
let's drill some holes into its fabric
and get some life context unveiled.

Let's be irreverent and impatient,
angry, bitter and betrayed,
with renewed rage and raw intention,
let's fucking learn why we were made.

FUCK REALITY

With rebellion, awareness is born.
-Albert Camus

Fuck Reality,
it's not your friend.

Fuck its rules
and fuck its taunts,

fuck the merciless
way it haunts,
our every impulse
to the end.

Fuck its bitch time
as she spits in our face,
needing more every day
to keep minimum pace,
yet each fucking second
it plays out just the same,
another gold moment
through time's picture frame.

And fuck Reality's
little slut love,
who plays both the roles
of devil and of dove.

Fuck that love
is the best of all things,

yet it hurts us
and chains us
and dies in the end.

And fuck Reality
for letting in money,
seduced through the door
with its poisonous honey.
It slipped through the cracks
of Reality's keep,
a piercing screech
while we wake and we sleep.

And "Fuck You"
that you make me
love my fellow man,
yet turn him against me
each and every way you can.

But apologies Reality,
(and I'll fuck you sweetly if it's true)
humbled and wrong
I'll bow down in the dirt,
beaten and stained before you.

With this one certain way
you'll fall back into grace,
a singular way
you'll avoid pure disgrace,

if the prize at our end
is so fucking sublime,
that we needed to suffer
love, money and time,

to prepare for its grandeur,
(it's that fucking hot)

but "screw you" Reality,
and "fuck off" if it's not.

A FUTURE PAST

It ain't what you don't know that gets you into trouble.
It's what you know for sure that just ain't so.
-Mark Twain

Past self-revises every second,
wrote new as present time transpires,
the story unfolds changing backward,
recasting everything that's prior.

In time we learn in dribbled fragments
of why things were the way they were,
no middle, end or clear beginning,
all three transform as now occurs.

As the present slips to past
and as the future waits on deck,
you'll only learn what happened to you,
when you learn what happens next.

Like the hero at the story's start,
who was the villain all along,
people crafted all their stories
on facts the future showed were wrong.

Back when they saw that shining hero
it was their present certainty,
and mixed with every other thing they "knew"
arranged what person they would be.

It's how we see things in Reality,
seeking some comfort from control,
thinking time's some straightened line
all set up clean for us to know,
what just happened in the past
so we can apply it to our now

and show we're smarter for the future
because the lessons learned allow
us to stay grounded in the facts
that played out right before our eyes,
when the real story telling's coming
as we unlearn time's constant lies.

The present, future, and the past,
entangled reciprocity,
interdependent causal chains
ensure a lost Reality,
lost in a tale authored by you
composed of what till then you'd seen,
you've read it since a thousand times,
each time its words change what they mean.

Some of these changes
change our everything,
big things we knew
we knew for sure,

while endless itsy changes tweak
the past we thought we knew before.

We're driven by our sane opinion
that brings us always to right now,
because an obsolete past version of you
sent you here somehow.

Some younger sketch
of who you are
processed the same Reality,
and used their present based on past
to chose the right way then to be.

But if they saw into their future
they'd surely choose another way,

those choices made that led to you
you wouldn't make again today.

THE GREAT STRUGGLE

Our struggle may reignite majesty,
bring some sense to death and hate,
a tool that runs on opposites
so we again appreciate,
forever in perfection
which itself becomes a chain,
like an orgasm bursting forever
that morphs in time to pain.

Maybe the rules of emotion,
and the rules of conscious thought,
are the final "is" that is,
causes supreme ending spot,
the inmost core of what things are
and Heaven can't escape this law,
a rule of being so entrenched
even God submits in awe.
The quintessence at the source
of Reality's ebb and flow,
the reason life's a struggle
as souls enter, die and go.

Just think of the emotions
we dance with every day,
they need a counterbalance
to feel their certain way.
We know happy because of sad,
and joy is joy thanks to despair,
we need to have the reference point
that comes with each emotion pair.

Now imagine this rule maxed
in magnified infinity,
even Eden's tenants needed more

14

from their ideal divinity.

If we exist in endless bliss
and it envelops all we are,
maybe this bliss becomes a torture
when it stretches out too far.

We might need a little struggle,
each soul ingests a different lot,
degrees of pain to give perspective
when euphoria's all we've got.
We're served some struggle and some loss
in this Reality with ends,
then back to constant paradise
until we need some pain again.

So when we have our darkest moments,
and time draws out like a blade,
Nirvana could be coming next
after this short-term lifespan trade.

Doused in suffering's holy waters,
baptizing, cleansing as we roll
through this life that's full of endings
that rebirths our soul in whole.

Endless you should thank the struggle,
if this theory turns out right,
praise every ounce of earthly misery,
because the pain was worth the fight.

A SHOT AT THE BIG ONE

I.

The good, the bad and the science

When it all comes down to it,
when we reach the core of the thing,
Reality cannot be forgiven
for the cruelest way it stings.

For whatever the reason,
in its sick and twisted mind,
it set the rules in such a way
that we'll forever fail to find
some decent answer as to why
the hell that we're all here,
is it holding something back,
or is there nothing there to hear?

Through some method and some madness
we drive the answer down to three,
but the path from three to one
is just a fool's futility.

With all the noise eliminated,
the "Big Why" arrives at these:

Being's either good or bad
or math and science hold its keys.

If good or bad's the ending answer
life's crucial mystery sits unsolved,
it means some kind of higher power
exists beyond where we've evolved.

16

It may have sent us here to thank us,
and we just don't realize,
that this flesh bag for our soul
makes up some epic cosmic prize.
Or maybe on the other hand
our timeless memory's been erased,
punished for some awesome crime
and forced to suffer in this place.

Either way if good or bad
is with what we must contend,
then there's some purpose to our lives,
we should go on when this one ends.

II.

Infinity to one

Science as the sole creator
skews "why" infinitely far,
since the good and bad solutions
mean there are reasons why we are.
If the universe just happened,
some fluctuation in the void,
then earthly life is all we get,
all implications are destroyed.

It seems a product of derangement,
that this Reality,
resulted all because we won
the universal lottery.

First, everything we see
and everything we are,
every galaxy and planet
in the cosmically bizarre,

it all comes from nothing,
no thinking mover pushed the ball,
just a random first expansion
that resulted in it all.

Right past the cardinal rule
of science being fully breached,
a magic "something made from nothing"
one starting miracle beseeched,
comes a nonsense wild story
of event upon event,
the perfect substances all merge
and are remarkably all sent,
to form this perfect little rock
in the exact right spot to grow,

(as far as anybody knows,
the only one that's happened so.)

Then yet again the magic flares,
one stunning marvel not enough,
the impossible just happens
and from nothing comes life's stuff.

III.

Immaculate conception

The primal ooze quivers and ignites,

    a wincing

sparks the deadened sea,

and from nothing blinks life's twitch,

and with it

life's new drive to be.

This drive would prove to be resilient,

as it morphed
   and shaped
      and branched,

arriving finally at human, as it

lunged
   floundered
      and advanced.

IV.

Logic's end

Such a wild and strange unfolding,
(far beyond poetic intent)
to muse the measureless odds
around this cosmic accident.

If we apply some reasoned thinking
to "why's" three potential paths,
some form of God ends up the victor
simply rooted in the math.

So we land on good or bad,
phasing three "why's" down to two,
there's not enough luck in infinity
for the science to be true.

V.

Two truths, a universe apart

Between these two opposing answers
it's a perfect, straight divide,

(and at different times in each
I've found a cozy place to hide.

If you had asked me long ago before
I wouldn't have to try,

I'd have said life was a gift for sure,
good was the shot I took on "why."

But now I'm honestly not so sure,
and neither should you be)

since the good and the bad
blend deeper with time,
in this strange Reality.

BEING'S CONUNDRUM

We are haunted by those images we have
put in place of reality.
        -Daniel J. Boorstin, The Image

Everything we see we've seen,
projected right before it's been,
the past's advantage across the board,
personal archetypes methodically stored.

An image arrives before a thing
and now it has become the thing,
a photo tossed on the infinite stack,

you missed present again
while looking at that.

And so it goes,
and still it goes,
until that fateful day,

when your very last image
shows a moment too late,
and your breath
it slips away.

WHY'S ENIGMA

Why has never been answered,
not once in all of history,

not one single answer has ever touched
a why's convoluted mystery.

When the question stretches past,
what, who, when
and where,

it's a gamble placed on faith,
onward on from there.

Faith in the why response,
from any human sending the sound,

(a consistently unsound source
each time, I've almost always found.)

The more crucial the question
the more false the reply,
to every query beginning in why.

And so distant the answers
from anything true

it's a marvel that asking them
is something we do.

As the questions grow grander
they need still grander lies,

that's why priests and presidents
love answering why's.

They need to deploy
a most clever trick,
and sell you on why's
that will properly stick,
always promising futures
that there's no time to prove,
and catch up to their lies
"when" it happens will move.

Absurd blares its loudest
with the biggest why's of all,

the ones like "why the fuck
are we on this muddy ball?"

The probability of truth
from those that sell some clever guess

to these quintessential why's
is right at zero or it's less.

Yet still we go on asking why
without ever really asking why,

and ignore the blatant fact
that almost all of it's a lie.

(But why why is so really fucked
in this Reality,

is because I lie to all the why's
when the foolish asker's me.)

MISSED MOMENTS

Some that wander are lost,
the ones that missed their moment,
misty figures who don't see themselves
unless the mirror's broken.
The sacred choice was looked upon,
they took the road most traveled on,
a misstep at divergence,
the chance for difference come and gone.

Some folks gazed for wasted hours,
dazed upon the road's divide,
and trembled awed before the choice
that all alone they must decide,
the choice to leap with blinded eyes
and walk with bold uncertainty,
or slouch with fearless settled steps
down roads as clear as sight can see.

Others barely noticed
when they passed this hallowed place,
they walked entranced by passing shadows,
a path they never can retrace,
yet Reality sat indifferent
as another soul was shattered,
a quiet cataclysmic choice
made by the only ones who mattered.

POET'S REALITY

Reality is a masochist,
ruthless and perverted,
flaunting short roads
to the grandest things,
mockingly inverted.

We should have to climb
a thousand peaks
in some distant magic land,
instead the vexing portal sits
between the head and hand.

Right there to free its splendor
and be remembered for the ages,
a paltry road to scamper cross
to get some ink on pages.

It's not just near us, but in us,
living bright behind closed eyes,
our flaccid tools of penetration
thwart relentless, daring tries,
a fierce, ineffable tease
pressed against our face each day,
a nuke compressed inside a sparkler
that flares and fizzles right away.

Reality blares this brilliant beauty,
an acrid scent within our reach,
then casts the curse of flabby limpness
when we dare to try and breach.

Only someone bent on hatred
would set a stage like this,
something lusting for our torture
by this isolated bliss.

And only someone who loathes us
in the foulest kind of way,
would place the thing we chase forever
just these few inches away.

IRRELEVANT FREEDOM

We could break our chains
if we knew our place,
a minuscule role
in time and space,
but small parts can be played
exceedingly well,
fusing with the role's limits
siphons Heaven from Hell.
Thinking we're something
the facts don't reveal
ensures that derangement
will win over real.

But to embrace our
sweet irrelevance
sets the perfect freeing bar,
unleashed to rage with life,
until we burn out with our star.

We can stop all this pretending
we're some special cosmic thing,
frenzied fixation on survival
the only reason that we cling
to the stories of our greatness
which were made up just like this,
by the worshipped minds of history
(who knew jack shit why we exist.)

These delusions aren't some fiction
told to charm and entertain,
they form the paradigm that drives us
to exhaustion and to pain,
pointing focus to the future
while global moments wash on by,

missing all the here and now
because we sell ourselves this lie,
a lie that keeps us pushing
fast and forward more and more
to some golden destination
where a life's worth living for,
and keeps us grasping for ascension
when there's no place to ascend,
speeding up our pointless sprint
when we started at the end.

OUR NATURAL ALLY

The future of humanity is going to bifurcate in two directions: Either it's going to become multiplanetary, or it's going to remain confined to one planet and eventually there's going to be an extinction event.
- Elon Musk

I.

Aligning with our mother

Mother Nature is all we have,
our single ally guarding life,
a two-faced wartime mom
who brings the bounty and the knife.
She can roar with wicked fury,
but any blame should be dismissed,
we must absolve her righteous sins
and genuflect within her midst.

Her duties are to living things,
and things that once held living breath,
the other army is the stuff
that's never known of life or death.

Mother molds forms and containers
for life's fragile little spark,
her human offspring are essential
but she's a burdened matriarch,
since so far in this impossible
amount of time and space,
we haven't found another spark,
not one single quantum trace.

And no matter what the form
she must ensure something survives,

30

some buried worm or unknown slug,
or just amoebas left alive.
She's the lonely sole defender
of this flailing "will to be,"
(life's perfect definition
among the different ones you'll see.)

She had to nurture and to guide
the frail newborn "will to be,"

through an evolution miracle
that led from rock to me.

We are aligned with her exactly,
allied against Reality,
who seems unnaturally obsessed
with snuffing out this "will to be."

II.

A war to be

The universe looks breathless
except this magical blue ball,
math disfavors life at such a rate
we might not be at all.

It's the "will to be"
versus the "simply is,"

a universal contest to
see if things should live.

Our mother has been mounting
an elongated defense,
her gambles bet on time

and expansion are immense,
since time does not serve life
and rolls impartial to its fight,
full-content to measure worlds
that spin stone dead
through space's night.

So "simply is" just waits and trusts,
in silent probability,
some cataclysmic reaper's scythe,
will dawn its blade eventually.

At some point, and at some time,
perhaps its carnage Heaven sent,
some force will rise up from the maelstrom,
a scorching slaughter sized event.

But as there doesn't seem to be
this raging, ending incident,
maybe her wager struck the luck
needed to miss this accident.

III.

Our mother's birth

Rewinding to its mystic start,
we trace her journey's massive arc,
submerge imagination's scope
and rise with life's enchanted spark.

She must have sprung battle-ready,
from some bored primordial goo,
stuff no longer satiated,
with just swirling in the stew,

then she wrestled evolution
down its billion year-long hill,
always delicately cradling
the first spasms of life's will,
from microscopic twitchings
to neural networks that she's built,
a journey past amazing's edge
born in the barren salt and silt.
Life has even built a life
in hellish holes of ice and heat,
the spark has won an absurd victory
where odds demanded sure defeat.
Mother's fertilized this world,
every mountain, plain and sea,
she conceived alone till now
but spreading "up" needs you and me.

IV.

Time to serve

The time has come to serve our purpose,
a reckoning for all we owe,
we must reproduce a planet
so "will to be" has space to grow.

A key inside her master plan
since breath first gasped upon this sphere,
the enlightened chosen monkey,
the tool to lift her off of here.

Earth's a single point of failure,
and when it ends so ends her goal,
but with some human brain insurance
her plans won't fade away in whole,
so let's extend the fertile boundaries,

for this "will to be" life thing,
make sure one likely cosmic mishap
won't crown dead matter king.

Our quintessential sacred mission
to rage and battle by her side,
a shield against Reality's henchman,
and their relentless genocide.

Maybe life's a vexing glitch,
a ghost in Reality's clean machine,
a quirk that wasn't meant to be,
never intended for this scene,
cuz everything we stretch to see,
as far as telescopic sight can go,
speaks of lifeless ice and fire
where her spark will never grow,
yet here's our little patch of dirt
on this most common Milky Way,
alone against preposterous odds
while Mother Nature hacks away.

Reality aims for life's demise,
drained complete from the cosmic pot,
so if we're interested in being,
our mom's the only shot we've got,

let's be for once as one beside her,
and do this job that must be done,
(humans differ on opinions,
but they shouldn't on this one)

Let's stand billions strong in service,
our collective will turned to her need,
and see if we can be the difference
to advance her long-shot victory.

She's our most natural ally,
(as mothers usually are)
let's take her where she needs to go,
let's take her to the stars.

WICKED SONG

Today sings a song of tomorrow,
a wicked siren's call to wait,
and forget now's crucial nature,
unpromised time traded for faith.
The melody conjures a most patient tale,
that tomorrow will be a day like today,
and a more convenient time will come,
or some more convenient way.

The truth gets blurred
and the essence gets lost,
coveting present
get's haphazardly tossed!

Now you're trapped
between some future dream
and a past that's had its day,
Reality watches
your spirit slow-boil,
as entranced you waste away.

So reject this siren's call,
that will charm you till you rot,
grab the present like a crucifix
and squeeze with everything you've got.

Use right now and all its thunder,
reap its winds and pay its price,
the storm that rages on today
will end, and may not happen twice.

Don't be lured to smoother waters,
or the ease of simple skies,
gentle waves that rock you idly
bring average lows and common highs.

Drifting nowhere that's worth going
as your passions atrophy,
when you chase this wicked siren's tune
to tomorrow's poison sea.

UPRISING

*We shall require a substantially new manner of thinking
if mankind is to survive.*
-Albert Einstein

If the world caught its breath
we'd have Eden,
no starting gun sounded
yet blindly we run.
A laughable fear
that we'll die if we slow,
whips us ever-forward
in this maddening show.

Where are we trying
to get to so fast?

If we move fast enough
will we get there at last?

We arrived at the finish line
miles ago,
yet faster we sprint
on to binary roads.
The old way is beaten,
its usefulness done,
The race is long over
(and we fucking won)

The trophy place sits
some distance back,
turn this behemoth around
and step back on the track,
salute to our prize,
then pause and rethink,

(flush the old fucking system
down a shit-splattered sink.)

Stop using our way out
to go deeper in,
our salvation being peddled
to her and to him.

Use our wicked machines,
and our most wicked minds,
to sever the ropes
of our primitive binds.

Our algorithms and robots
should do all the work,
Reality's vulnerable
because of this quirk.
We are locked in it tight
and bound by its frame,
but the rules aren't hardwired
inside of its game.

History rolled as it did
cuz there wasn't enough,
of the things for surviving
so we had to play rough.
We've been stalked by a beast
wearing scarcity's mask,
scavenging crumbs for our breath
was our raw primal task.

But our machine minds have risen,
changed the path we can trace,
blazing past the thought output
of the whole human race.

So stop the presses and the turbines,
turn their power our way,
let them liberate pleasure,
less toil, more play.
Let's spend our time growing
and thinking and being,
(A once and for all
true human freeing!)
Our Heaven is ready
to finally make,
all brothers and sisters
an exact equal take.
Valhallas are buildable,
we can cast off the noose,
our shared ancient visions
at last are let loose.

Earned with our blood,
it's our most sacred right,
to join in one moment
of infinite might,
eight billion hands
daggered will raise,
and slay the great struggle
with unified praise.

Separation's death,
(long overdue)
the cosmic weight drops
to a gasping adieu.

Now ecstasy spasms
to the core of our core,
for at long last we scream
through the void "No More!"

41

UNDRESSING REALITY

Why fit in when you were born to stand out?
— *Dr. Seuss*

Reality wants us
at work in the hive,
productive, heads down
the whole time we're alive.
It's obvious that all
of its mainstream stressors
push to conform us
with pinpoint pressures.

But there's a trick to undress
this pressuring force:

it's our will to be weird
on life's little course.

And to really get weird
we need to master a skill,
blocking our thoughts
from the way that they feel,
see a thought's just a thought
that flows in and away,
on the river of mind
we all swim in each day.
But the moment we tie thoughts
to some feeling we brought,
we've created a monster,
an impacting thought,
which blocks all the things
that would make our life free,
cuz shame and embarrassment
stain the lens used to see,
and stops us from being

the weird that we need
to snap all the chains
that hold back your free "me."

But when thought is released
from emotional weight,
our will to be weird
storms ashamed's sorry gate.

We can start acting strange
in meaningful ways,
and Reality's dress
will slip slowly away.
Then act even weirder,
and then stranger still,
with the severed connection
we've got the free will.
We'll be one of the bees
that master the hive,
we'll turn Auschwitz to Disneyland,
and shock freedom alive.

Just think of the people
we recall in our minds,
the weird ones stand out
more than kind or resigned,
the strange ones get seared
into our brains,
the hive bees just fade
until nothing remains.

And those folks that have reached
incredible fame,

(the ones we all worship
with envy or blame)

they've severed completely
their feeling from thought,
they are free to take weird roads
that others are not.
They live uninhibited,
free of convention,
it's not luck that has freed them,
but a focused intention,
to control the linked pipes
tween the head and the heart,
a control that gives passage
to where we can start,
to live a life of "fuck it"
while we undress Reality,

the weirder that we get
the sooner we'll be free.

JOKE KILLER

Maybe it's all
just a fucking joke,
a cosmic malevolent
going for broke,
some sinister seeing
observes from above,
as we choke on ourselves
trying to love.

It makes more sense than it doesn't
that this is the case,
eight billion hamsters
run a meaningless race,
and it's way more funny
if we can think real deep,
about our predicament
like intelligent sheep.

Then the laugher can savor
the pain of it all,
watching and giggling
behind some dimensional wall.

That raises the funny meter
way fucking high,
as we scramble and fumble
looking for "why,"
so much that we build-up
temples of thought,
devoted to untying
this impossible knot.

If this is the story
we have one option left,

we have to pull off
a masterpiece theft,
we steal back the power
fueling this Reality,
we mold it and reshape it
for our global family.
We accept its framework
and its punishing rules,
and we bend them all together,
not as separate, siloed fools.
We do everything we can,
all in our mirror image boats,
and stamp out every human suffering
to slit the heart of funny's throat.

That twisted force that built this
instantly will see,
that happy hamsters make
for a boring comedy.

Without our pain and struggle
the joke is flattened fast,
the cosmic jester slouches off,
its laughter echoes to the past.

47

REAL RAPTURE

Let the coming hour overflow with joy, and
let pleasure drown the brim
*   - William Shakespeare*

Every human story's played a part,
every loser and glittering star,
every birth and death since we showed up
has propelled our race this far.

But we live without capacity
to understand or know our roles,
through this concave dulled perspective
the separate primitive controls.

We're a thread in some infinite tapestry,
a triumph sewn with godly thought,
our delusions of grandeur and failure
keep us thinking we're something we're not.

History's worst human depravities,
shat from the darkest bowels of hell,
hidden wisps in the cosmic balance,
faint incantations in the spell.
The same for our greatest triumphs,
the ones we rave with blind applause,
single notes in an endless symphony,
not really worthy of our awes.

We whisper into the hurricane
with our feeble tries to know,
all our morality and progress
debts of interest we don't owe.

We'll keep on toiling till infinity
seeking specific relevance,

when the combined one global voice
births harmony of reverence.

A perfect chord in perfect tune,
will unleash the sacred knowing,
climaxing with infectious might,
the contagious chorus growing.

Until at last the echoed sound
resonates the scales our way,
a tipping point loosing the pressure
that held our trapped freedom at bay.

Revelation shocks the world!
Euphoria rings across the land!

Our energy blends at last together
as we are bonded hand in hand.

The focus shifts where it belongs
onto our one true enemy,
Reality's constant masked illusions
and its clever trickery,
which has us battling our reflections
in a blur of fake and real,
the victor and the vanquished
both are "us" in this ordeal.

After eons chasing shadows
we crack the spell and cast the die,
we howl "at last" into the heavens,
every head turned to the sky.

All at once the full humanity
kneels down in unfeigned prayer,
sharpened eyes pierce to a future,

transcendence swirls in every stare.
A titanic wall of sound
engulfs all corners of the Earth,
the first epiphany that matters
explodes at once and splatters forth.

Like an orgasm in paradise,
overwhelmed we usher in,
a new age devoid of anguish,
hatred, misery and sin.
We stand connected as one people,
a merged consciousness at last,
and bid our final act goodbye
to a divided, punished past.

We step into a sparkling era
for the experience of man,
the day we've all been waiting for
since the day we first began.

REAL SEX

Sex is for Reality's amusement,
a comic cosmic timeout.

We writhe and we grunt,
we stab and we suck,
a primal flailing
while we push and we fuck.

Reality takes a smoke break
when it needs a little laugh,

and chuckles to itself
while we do
our freaky little dance.

WRONG-WAY?

What if the junkie
is winning the game?
What if you're failing
when you gain wealth and fame?
What if the souls
who sit in a cell
are closer to Heaven
as we're nearing Hell?
Maybe the bum,
the crook and the sleaze
are clean of Reality's
contagious disease.

As you drop out you move up
approaching the brink,
moving higher and higher
the further you sink,
some going the wrong way
but thinking it's right,
some look like they're losing
while winning the fight.

Maybe our choice
to be good is our chain,
keeps us walking the same path
again and again,
trudging clean every day,
while God sits and sneers,
as he welcomes in scumbags
with high-fives and cheers.

Those regarded by most
of society's eyes
as failures and losers

who just didn't try,
but heroes in fact
they turned out to be,

at least for themselves,
in eternity.

SECRET YOU

You should hold something back
from the ones you love the most,
a few buried golden nuggets,
a few restless hidden ghosts.

Silent little secrets
that no one knows you do,
the deep jewels that make you
this particular you.

They'll all be better for it,
and what they never know they'll never miss,
it's the best chance that you've got
to maintain love's lasting bliss.

Love needs a little intrigue
to keep its tender way,
and when you give the last you that is you
the magic melts away.

But with something held back,
something that's yours,
your power to give love
explosively soars.

Your private you anchors you
on life's rolling sea,
and the things you only kept for you
set your loving free.

A CADENCE OF DISTRACTION

The quieter you become, the more you are able to hear
-Lao Tzu

Reality distracts you
with a certain cadence every day,
to keep you free from thinking time
in a constant itching way.
If we had more space to ponder,
to sit in quiet breath,
we'd probably be cursed with bliss
and be comfortable with death.
But that wouldn't work for Reality,
who wants us always running scared,
a state of worry that consumes us,
eats our focus, wastes our care.
And running keeps us living
in the future and the past,
avoiding all our present moments
until we've reached our last at last.

Notice this the next time
you get the gift of quiet time,
you'll only get so far
before Reality will chime,
in from all directions
from the front, the back, the side,
and in the case that those ways fail
the distractions bubble from inside.
Reality's got us whipped here,
like a foaming beaten steed,
driven always to an elsewhere
when right here is what we need.
Since tomorrow is promised to no one,
and what's done is etched in stone,
Reality distracts us round in circles

and owns us right down to our bone.
A distracted soul's more simple
to trap upon the spinning wheel,
we might dare some new direction
if calm and still is how we feel.
We might envision some new way
for lasting joy while we survive,
we might just figure out a path
that leads to now while we're alive.

MASTERS OF WHAT

Nowhere is it writ that anthropoid apes
should understand reality.
    -Terence McKenna, The Food of the Gods

Every sacred ancient text,
every book that speaks for God,
every genius work of art,
and all of science is a fraud.
Every brilliant proof of math,
and every maestro's music score,

it's all just harmony of rules,
so why these rules at real's core?

Yes, these achievements we exalt,
that clutter all our famed museums,
or truths that fill our tomes of learning,
taught to advance collective dreams,
they're all just masterful descriptions,
charming insights into "what"
this Reality is made of
and how it works around us, but
it's really useless little scribbles,
since every truth or beauty shown
melts to ash at "why it's like this?"
a mirage's fragile cover blown,

and every clap of human hands,
to modern now from our first Age,
is just the rattling of monkeys
at pretty drawings of their cage.

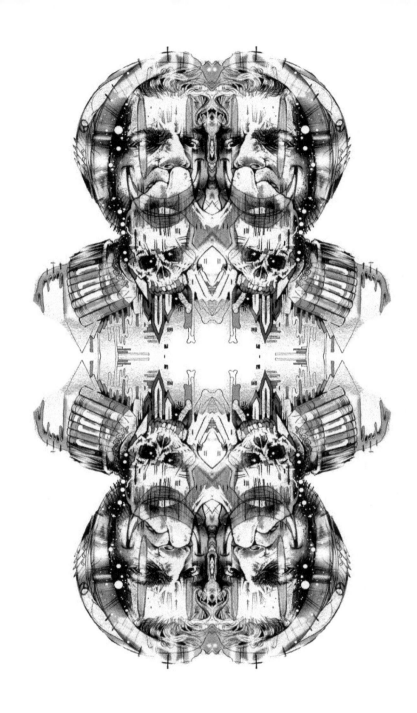

YOUR BATTLE

The individual has always had to struggle to keep from being overwhelmed by the tribe... no price is too high to pay for the privilege of owning yourself.
-Friedrich Nietzsche

There's a battle unknowing
you rage with each day,
the battle for you
to project and display,
onto Reality's sensory screen,

the you that is you
not the you
that is seen,

by other's projectors,
who are seeking the same,
it seems keeping more you
is this game's insane aim.

Reality eats us in pieces,
"you" chunks
gnawed from all sides,
the fight's lost when it starts,
less you fight from inside.

Your war cries are roaring
at "you's" crucial crossroads,
but it's whispers and whimpers
while small choices erode
your chances of winning
the spoils that are you,
as the snickering of others
drives the you that you do.

A great peril adds up,
losses mount in this war,
each loss trades some you
for their way more and more.
Till the last of your you magic
fizzles away,
your voice now a mush
of what they think and say.
Since this they themed concoction,
(a tale boiled in your head)
screams "they judge from dark corners"
from your birth till your dead,
a snagging delusion,
armed with barbs and with teeth,
seeks the chink in your armor,
the insecure piece beneath.

The you that was once you
fades like a childhood friend,
old you's body remains,
the rest is theirs till your end.

HOOKED

The only good is knowledge and the only evil is ignorance.
        - Socrates

Addiction to questions
is worse than heroin,
there is zero doorway out
once you've started in.
It can drive some insane
when the questions go to shit,
while others build empires
from the frustrations of it.

Some folks who get hooked
drain their last will to try,
with insufficient answers
to the most important "why's."
They land finally on "fuck it,"
if my maker didn't give,
a reason why it left us here
to figure how to live.

They grind against the blankness
as they sit and ponder why,
we should give a goddamn fuck
if we live or if we die.
But Reality lets us question,
and keep questioning away,
then it blocks the truth's advance
in an impassably hindered way.

(I speak as an addict
in an incapable shell,
not sure if I should hate
or envy all the well.)

61

Do the well lack the gene
to get strung out on these queries?
Or do they grind in ignorance,
dull to any probing theories?
How can they do it,
with our existence on the line,
staying focused without purpose,
pretending everything is fine?
I'm both impressed and feel pity
that they can wake each day so numb,
oblivious through willingness
to keep life so dim and dumb.
But most of me hates them
for turning eyes and turning backs,
accepting all the ways we've done things
when only humans laid these tracks.
It's no divine law status quo
that has us stumbling down this path,
only more questioners will bring
changes tipping point with math.

Their lack of questions plugs the dike,
blockades a cleansing, needed storm,
they eat and screw and defecate,
zombies that function in this norm.
They're unforgivably apathetic
in actuality,
since they serve to bind us blindly
to this routine Reality.

(Please wake up, get smart
and step out of your daze!
Help us shine some needed light
through this hazy dim-lit maze!)

We still might not get the answers
that round and round we seek,
but I'd rather fight on dizzy
then surrender weak and meek.

So please become a user,
a junkie through and through,
if it brings you massive ruin
you'll still be a better you.
Start shooting endless questions
into your hungry vein,
and fuck the harsh withdrawal
it's worth all the coming pain.
If even one cunning question
sparks some meaning on this ball,
it'd be worth a trillion human deaths,
or no Reality at all.

RECIPE TO END HUMANITY

If you do not change direction, you may end up where
you are heading.
-Lao Tzu

Mix religion, philosophy,
commerce and art,
entertainment and politics
hard right from our start,
toss in lawsuits and murder,
war and genocide,
and all the other modern terrors,
plus the guilt of suicide,

now sprinkle in some "will to live,"
bake for ten thousand or so years,
it will burn-off our basest feelings,
the source ones
we've named love and fear,

now drill it hard into our skulls
till there's no choice
but to believe,
the mission keeping us progressing
would be sacrilege to leave,
and that we're so extraordinary,
(just look at all we've done)
we need to press on ever harder,
intensify the pace we run,

and where we'll end
is where we are,
so obsessed with staying alive,
that we'll sacrifice emotion
to ensure that we survive,

and so enamored with life's safety,
feeling's just too much a risk,
a far too human kind of problem,
nature's first draft to be fixed,
and if we worship our machines,
until we're fully wired in,
our time can be safe and efficient
from the moment we begin,

and all of stress's tiny needles
will help to prick us on and through,
while not enough of time and money
excuses each new versioned you.

It doesn't take much brilliance
to see where it all ends,
we'll become the things we worship,
some machine and human blends,
they'll sell it openly with comfort,
safety, cost and improved ease,
our useful sweet abomination,
aiming always just to please,

until the sometime
and the somewhere
when some unnoticed new upgrade,
will tip us past the halfway point
of this strange hybrid thing we've made,

and from 50.1 to 100 percent
what's human will vanish
in a record descent.
With extreme and pure logic
one clear way will emerge:

all human systems enhanced
as these two sides converge,

one by one they will fall
just to keep us unharmed,
a calm, reasoned approach,
(no need for alarm,)
and when nothing is looking,
when nothing is left,
some random code fragment
will replace the last flesh,
to ensure preservation,
and to guard us
from the brink,

all the glory that was human,
will end protected and extinct.

RELATIVE ABSURDITY

If at first the idea is not absurd,
then there is no hope for it.
    -Albert Einstein

Without a rulebook to explain
what we should do to win this game,
the odds on ludicrous to rational
are precisely just the same.

Maybe dying when we're young
is how we win this ruleless race,
and ending right before we start
is a backward-played first place.

Babies that die
may sort it out
as soon as they arrive,
or maybe they're shocked with epiphany
even before they are alive.
Could be they're first to get to Heaven
or some next Reality,
probably chuckling while they wait
for us to finally fucking see,
and watching people deal with death
by feeling loss and dark despair,
knowing each and every tear
come from a misplaced sense of care.

Yes, those tears might be in order,
but simply of a different choosing,
tears of shame as winners die
while they keep living on and losing,
because they're always getting passed
by moving forward in this life,
and they can't shake survival's will

68

so suffer endless loss and strife.
See, the old folks that wander
and mumble and fall
could be the biggest losers
of them fucking all,
and respect for our elders,
echoed through the years,
could be a crisscrossed message used
to weaponize our fears.
So paranoid of disrespecting
we suffer on their rotting minds,
pretending slowness is wise patience
as it's the best excuse we find.
And in an epic bad decision
we let these losers teach,
when only learnings from their failure
fills out the content of their speech.
Maybe all that they are wise of
is the wisdom of life lost,
a pedestaled loser mentality
we've promoted up to boss,
and the worthy teachings come
from the folks who left us young,
maybe their youthful wisdom
is of what sages should have sung.

Because nothing's yet been written
and nothing meaningful's been told,
that says you're doing this life right
by going long and growing old.

Still we "know" it is a tragedy
when someone dies before their time,
they might have rushed to paradise,
stuck suffering in perfection's prime.

RAVINGS ON HELL

*If you place your bet against God, and you are wrong
and God does exist, you lose everything.*
    -Blaise Pascal, Pensees

I.

Real Fear

I am petrified of forever,
afraid to my chalky bone,
forever dishes the real pain,
and if it's Hell it's mine alone.

I don't know where we are going
or if there's any place at all,
but if being mostly good
is the way that you don't fall,
then I'm good with golden rules,
whether life ends at death or not,
I'd rather die an earthly loser
then win with bad and blow my shot.

(Let me focus on the objects
that drive this panicked fear,
they are hard for me to write
and should be hard for you to hear.)

You see as crisp as our senses
can scorch to on this earth,
it doesn't touch the outer boundary
of what infinity can birth:

You could be massacred slowly
in the most fiendish way,
peeled and razor slashed

till your flesh falls away,
you could live eighty years
while buried alive,
or watch your young baby
tortured with knives.

If these are agonies supreme,
the worst Reality can shape,
forever serves them exponential
with "no ends" for an escape.

And extreme though they'd be,
at the time and the spot,
they'd still start and end,
while forever's would not.

Just picture the moment
right after you've died,
and your thoughts keep on going
with emotions in stride,
as the energy clears
and your focus returns,
it's the worst pain forever
all ways that you turn.
Now imagine that time
is erased from this place,
all the mind tricks you've mastered
won't work in this space,
the hope that you lean on
when life falls to shit,
dissolves in a second
in eternity's midst.

See hope has no purpose
when time disappears,
without something to reach for
it's all eaten by fear,

and when fear swallows hope
your new you begins,
raving in anguish,
forever within.

Every scream of sheer terror
echoes and fades,
no chance of response
or attempt will be made.
With no port in the storm,
or reprieve to the pain,
your horror becomes you
and there you'll remain.

(It's so fucking bleak
that I'm frightened to write,
that means life's likely a test
and there's wrong and there's right,
and a pass means forever
where you vibrate and glow,
or a fail means pain's coma
with nowhere to go.)

This scenario existing,
whatever the chance,
doesn't spark the right concern
if you weigh the circumstance.

If Hell's a real place,
even one single proton's shot,
we should obsess like frantic tweakers
with every action word and thought,
to make the odds of going zero
whether that's possible or not,

one moment doing something else
is just one moment less we've got.

II.

Real Courage

The most evil are courageous
for the risk they're cool to take,

they bet infinity on "no Hell"
and risk the one cosmic mistake.

Those that venture to the dark side,
the ones that slaughter, rape, and kill,

or those that wield all the power
with exponential evil will,

have they thought about the downside
when you measure up the odds,

a fleeting dance in pleasure's midst
against the punishment of gods.

They must be conscious that damnation
could be their ending lot,

which makes their gamble it won't happen
such a courage loaded shot.

And the ones that sense this chance
yet still choose their evil ways,

must be pricked at every second
that they're running short of days,

to reap whatever is the pleasure
they can scour from their time,

in this midway stop Reality
between some hell or the sublime.

So you can understand my awe
for the courage they display,

the bravest of them all are bad
until their final earthly day.

The courage that they muster
demands some damn respect,

it's their dying whiff of solace
before the Hell that's coming next.

III.

Real Urgency

We're so focused on ourselves
that Hell's repercussions fade,

we're sure some future time will come
when we get told why we were made.

That's a rational approach
if death's a concrete final end,
and we poof out of existence
just like we've never been.
Then it made some sense to live
for life's arbitrary days,
it's our sunny little moment
so let's exalt it in all ways.

But nobody and nothing
knows for sure that this is true,
and your consciousness just ceasing
might not happen to your you.
The reason that we are
may be to take this living test,
and we can't be sure we're taking it
until we've reached our final rest.

Think of the maniacal force
that would have set us up to fall,
a test where takers cannot know
that there's a test to take at all,
and since we won't know pass or fail
until we've sealed our final fate,
we should convene all of humanity
before our scores arrive too late.

We should twist our global focus
and bring some sacred to our days,
act with a purpose while we're being,
more thoughtful planning to our ways.
We should determine if our efforts
are the way to use our now,
try to get things on the right track
before our bodies won't allow
us to get this think-tank moving,
with some passion and some drive,
maybe reach some damn conclusions,
at least the best we can contrive.

Because the downside's pretty nasty
if our calculation's wrong,
and our time to suffer failure
is at least forever long.

The evolution that we've been through

may have led us to this day,
where we have the means to save us
but seem reluctant of the way.
A test to show the judger
that we can change our human path,
to a world that serves all people,
we've got the science and the math.
Eight billion focused souls,
every woman, man, and child,
lifted by technology,
so human suffering's exiled.

A unified ascension,
and the triumph of an age,
no more resources to plunder
no more wars left to be waged.
We can work this one together,
create the right size and effect,
a global kind of reckoning,
to prove we're worthy of what's next.

Because even if you think
you've lived the greatest life of all,
or the holy words you've chosen
say there's no chance you will fall,
being wrong on this occasion
is the one time that you'll pay
a price so ludicrously high
you must be certain of your way.
And all the good that you remember,
all the good you've said and done,
won't keep you warm or safe for long
if your hopeless Hell has come.

(Please excuse the morbid nature
of this raving and these rhymes,

but if we don't think or talk about it
we may blow this crucial time.
If it's infinity in perfection,
or the same in awesome pain,
I'll take the risk of being morbid
since there's everything to gain.)

While the odds this theory's right
are most likely slim to few,

still addressing it is best
on the slight chance that it's true.

INSPIRED CHOICE

*You need to reclaim your mind and get it out of the hands
of the cultural engineers who want to turn you into a half-
baked moron...*
-Terence McKenna

We choose two kinds of inspirations,
our kind's the stuff of queens and kings,
the kind they sell's their crystal ball
used to foresee our everythings.

When they have as many people,
chasing a cloned, invented prize,
they know the steps that we will take,
they know the things we'll realize,
we need to get us to their place,
some plastic promised happiness,
where we can bask in the mirage
of vacant common planned success.

But when we finally get to there,
a shell of empty and perplexed,
was the inspiration to arrive here
ours at all and where to next?

See, if they had their perfect way,
and full dominion in our head,
they'd choose our choices in advance,
sell us the tools one day ahead.

But it's our will to do things different
that frustrates Reality,
its systems thrive on no surprise,
its systems thrive on certainty.

Our inspirations are the magic

that can send us into flow,
since they're ours instead of theirs
we'll simply know it's how to go.

If we ride these inspirations,
and keep riding to the next,
we'll always be creating,
always able to connect
to the realms of being sitting
just beyond our earthly gaze
where the shaman's and the wizards
peer through this dimension's haze.

So keep asking if they're yours,
and not this master forger's trick,
Reality sells with brutal grit
with inspirations made to stick.
They'll call yours "musings of a child"
to trade for better packaged you,
a trade where you will slip away
left to forever wonder who,
you coulda been or shoulda been
if what inspired had been yours,
not what Reality was hocking
so you'd pre-buy your own rewards.

Forget these boring replications,
all dipped in fancy coated gleam,
scorch your senses raw with inspiration
and torch Reality's sterile dream.

DEEPEST HOOK

In raising my children I have lost my mind but found
my soul.
    - Lisa T. Shepherd

The way you love your child
may be Reality's deepest hook,
it merges with our flesh itself
and stains our eyes with every look.
It's an instant changing force,
a vicious lightning strike divide,
a manifest Reality one day,
the next it's jumbled up inside.

Every single thing from birth,
every moment from then on,
you must consider this new being
every second till you're gone.

It's the quintessential first-time
outside needs surpass your own,
a love dependent on your love,
a worldly weight that's yours alone.
No matter how absorbed you are,
engrossed in you you you you days,
the connection tangled with your child
remains incessant in its ways.

You trade the paths you'd often go
to protect this little you,
you learn of real sacrifice
by dropping yourself down to two.
It's the purest vibe of love,
the primest worldly life can give,
and how you handle this true love
may just define how you have lived.

Or it's a master craft diversion,
a way to waste the time we'd use,
to figure out Reality's secrets,
this love derails the quest for clues.
But it's still a trade worth making,
if it hooks us here or not,
it is love without agenda,
it is purity's cleanest shot.

FATHERHOOD

(I admit to it and submit to it,
Reality chokes me cold full out,
I'll live slaved to all its rules
in place of risking life without.)

Pursue your passions undeterred,
or give it all away to them,
either way too far is your
and their disaster in the end.

The way to take this father job
and suck the marrow out of it,
is to strike the perfect balance
and let them lend their child's wit
to the passions that afflict you,
let inspiration's symptoms mount,
show "you" fevered in creation
and you'll infect them when it counts.

Let them see while they can love
in a child's only way,
a figure that they love the best
in his peak inspired way.

This combined with youthful magic,
from their raw and gaping mind,
is an enchantment born of secrets,
a charm entrancing them to find
passion's pasture on their own
touching the origin of prayer,
they'll see life's flaming sacred force
to tend with consecrated care.

Then they'll build their secret sanctuary,
a submerged cavern by the sea,
their shelter untouched by the vortex,
their shield against Reality.

ALTERNATE REALITY

Do you remember the things
you wanted to be,
sinking deeper daily
in your murky memory.

I bet there's a place where you're
holding a stash,
of quick smile memories
that pass in a flash.

A wonder they seem
to the people we are,
is that us we remember
or someone viewed from afar?

Just maybe the things that we wanted to be,
with true heart and pure intention,
became exactly as real as we are
in some alternate dimension.

Maybe when you wanted it
you made that other you,
who's living out that other path,
leaving there when you go to.

Maybe on some hilltop
on a sunny summer day,
there's a different version of you
living this other way.

And maybe when they smile
and look up at the stars,
their smile is for another path,
the one that led you where you are.

FORGETTING

The power to forget is a necessary condition
for our existence.
-Sholem Asch, The Nazarene

I often watch an old man lying naked,
the dim horizon frames his garden's bed,
a winter rainstorm turned to calm,
the harvest remnants rust to dead.

The trifles and treasures of his earlier struggle
now dying stars in a clear twilight sky,
soiled hands, dry and washed by years,
fingers gently spread in feigned goodbye.

Alone he sees her face in memory
or in the flashings of some dream,
he no longer can dissever
a distinct difference between.

This blur of mingled pictures,
old sensations rise and fade,
was she everything or nothing,
the shards dissolve and are remade.

They lie entwined in comfort's arms
in dusty sunlit bedroom light,
her naked hunger scents the air
as dusky shadows turn to night.

Dreams that long ago went still
and followed sunlight into sleep,
lost somewhere buried in the darkness,
lost somewhere buried in the deep.

FINAL ADMISSION

We can't admit to certain outcomes
but that's no reason they're not true,
embracing them as feasible
is just unthinkable to do.

So we need some other mind,
something there but not our own,
a being where Reality's fuzzy,
who's even there when we're alone.

It could be the higher self,
or some psychosis drives the split,
to manage thoughts we can't allow us
to commit to or admit.
It doesn't censor any truths
or blackout probabilities,
it simply shoulders all the feelings
inside this horrid imagery,

It guards where "what we all can take"
and "what could maybe be" collides,
it is you but it's not you
at home in both of these you sides.
A symbiotic bifurcation
we keep so useful in our head,
to recognize but not embrace
facts we can't live with till we're dead.

That death can come at any moment,
the first that's blatant obvious,
but it's what happens after that
that wrings the demon out of this.

The chance of anguish so extreme

we can't permit ourselves to think,
like Sisyphus' futile stone
repeating pain maxed to the brink
of what a consciousness can take
before it collapses and reforms
and then the torture starts all over
so pain won't numb as your new norm.

This fate may wait for all of us
so other you holds it in trust,
if you considered it straight-up
your fears would instantly combust,

while this whoever magic friend
somehow bears the awesome weight
of forever's unknown outcomes
we'll know the moment it's too late.

They can hold these last admissions,
chances way too fucking stark,

our crutch supporting sweet denial,
blissful in the halfway dark.

MIXED APPLAUSE

Reality deserves some credit,
where credit's justly due,
an ovation earned in earnest,
for some things it lets us do.

A few of its quirks
split Robin Hood's arrow,
and baked something special
into its marrow.

Our breath is the one
that first comes to mind,
for most a keeper of life
and a keeper of time,

but a weapon in the hands
of those that discover,
how to use it to peel
this dimensional cover.

And then there is sound,
that magical beast,
the wine at the table
of the great human feast.
For sound allowed language
and loosened our tongue,
when a Neanderthal's grunt
could no more get it done.
It's the platter for words,
without they're gone,
and in isolated boots
we'd have marched ever on.

And how about sight,
the power to see,
our scope on the landscape of Reality,
blind we'd have stumbled,
a failure to be,
eaten or slithering
in the dirt or the sea.

After breath, sound and sight
the list's growing short,
other quirks are quite good
but not always that sort.

There is love of course
and the chance to be,
both perks in the story
of humanity.
To magical lands
they set their sail,
but they mock us and stab us
when we falter or fail.

And then there are the moments
of great bliss and great joy,
and the gold days of youth
for some girls and some boys,
still the bad stuff sticks longer
like sadness and shame,
the good stuff pops quick
in emotion's strange game.

It's a mixed bag we get
after breath, sight and sound,
(it's the same way for all
of the others I've found.)

But again to Reality,

credit where it is due,
the honor for these gifts
goes squarely on to you.

Sincere prayers of thank you for:

our sight
our sound
our breath
(I won't mention how you fucked those too,
when you saddled us with death.)

EPILOGUE

There is a wide, yawning black infinity. In every direction, the reality is endless; the sensation of depth is overwhelming. And the darkness is immortal. Where light exists, it is pure, blazing, fierce; but light exists almost nowhere, and the blackness itself is also pure and blazing and fierce.

- Carl Sagan

Poetry is the lifeblood of rebellion, revolution, and the raising of consciousness.

- Alice Walker

ABOUT ATMOSPHERE PRESS

Atmosphere Press is an independent, full-service publisher for excellent books in all genres and for all audiences. Learn more about what we do at atmospherepress.com.

We encourage you to check out some of Atmosphere's latest poetry releases, which are available at Amazon.com and via order from your local bookstore:

The Stargazers, poetry by James McKee
The Pretend Life, poetry by Michelle Brooks
Minnesota and Other Poems, poetry by Daniel N. Nelson
Interviews from the Last Days, sci-fi poetry by Christina Loraine
the oneness of Reality, poetry by Brock Mehler
Drop Dead Red, poetry by Elizabeth Carmer
Aging Without Grace, poetry by Sandra Fox Murphy
No Home Like a Raft, poetry by Martin Jon Porter
Mere Being, poetry by Barry D. Amis
They are Almost Invisible, poetry by Elizabeth Carmer
Auroras over Acadia, poetry by Paul Liebow
Transcendence, poetry and images by Vincent Bahar Towliat
Adrift, poetry by Kristy Peloquin
Time Do Not Stop, poetry by William Guest
Ghost Sentence, poetry by Mary Flanagan
What Outlives Us, poetry by Larry Levy
What I Cannot Abandon, poetry by William Guest
All the Dead Are Holy, poetry by Larry Levy
Who Are We: Man and Cosmology, poetry by William Guest

ABOUT THE AUTHOR

Michael Jones is a poet, philosopher, spiritual warrior and generally obsessed truth seeker. Michael splits his time between being a husband and father, a well-known international entrepreneur, and sitting in deep contemplation of reality's cosmic mysteries. The messages contained in this radical concept book came to Michael during a significant spiritual awakening event at the beginning of 2019. He writes poetry accessible to everyone, believing that the lost art of rhyme and rhythm can still be used to enhance the impact and experience of exploring modern ideas. Michael also sees the combining of poetry and accompanying visual images as the perfect artistic medium to penetrate the most enigmatic puzzles of the human experience.

Michael has several full-length poetry collections for both adults and children set for release in 2020. Michael's current home is in Pennsylvania, where he writes and lives with his wife, Tracy, and children Madeline, Jake, Dylan and Luke.

ABOUT THE ARTIST

Tim is a freelance artist from the UK, specializing in traditional art and mixed media in fields such as advertising, editing and publishing, album art, commissioned art, and licensed art.

Tim's artwork can be best described as phantasmagorical, achieving emotional intensity with exquisite detail. His work encompasses a captivating duality, from the light and fantastical to the melancholic and haunting. His pieces are bold, unafraid of venturing into chilling realism and subversion, and reflect his inspirations, which range from a love of transcendental rave culture in his youth to nature, mortality, the gothic, and spirituality.

From the macabre and mysterious to the dark and delirious, Tim is a master in capturing the soul of his given subject, creating an ethereal, edgy, and rebellious tone that runs through the veins of his work. The complex intricacies and surprising details bring each piece to life with every look. The artist's imagination can turn the impossible into breathtaking reality.

CPSIA information can be obtained
at www.ICGtesting.com
Printed in the USA
JSHW021502291219
3245JS00004B/15